TRUE

True Hip-Hop
© Mike Schreiber

Design: Christopher D Salyers

This book is typeset in Caslon.

Without limiting the rights under copyright reserved above, no part of this publication may be used, reproduced, stored, transmitted or copied in any form or by any means (electronic, mechanical, photocopying, recording or otherwise) without prior written permission, except in the case of short excerpts embodied in critical articles and reviews.

Every effort has been made to trace accurate ownership of copyrighted text and visual materials used in this book. Errors or omissions will be corrected in subsequent editions, provided notification is sent to the publisher.

Library of Congress Control Number: 2010931563

Printed and bound in China through Asia Pacific Offset

10 9 8 7 6 5 4 3 2 1   First Edition

All rights reserved.

This edition © 2010
Mark Batty Publisher, LLC
36 West 37th Street, Suite 409
New York, NY 10018, USA.
Email: info@markbattypublisher.com
www.markbattypublisher.com

ISBN: 978-1-9356131-1-4

Distributed outside North America by
Thames & Hudson Ltd.
181A High Holborn
London WC1V 7QX
United Kingdom
Tel: 00 44 20 7845 5000
Fax: 00 44 20 7845 5055
www.thameshudson.co.uk

TRUE HIP-HOP

photography by Mike Schreiber

MARK BATTY PUBLISHER
NEW YORK CITY

CONTENTS

34	56	78
Young Buck	Juvenile	RZA
36	58	79
Dwele	C. Murder	Redman
38	60	80
muMs	B.G.	Jermaine Dupri
40	62	82
Maino	David Banner	Diddy
42	64	84
Juelz Santana	Lil Wayne	Voletta Wallace
44	66	86
Nas	Petey Pablo	Fat Joe
46	68	88
Black Star	Young Jeezy	State Property
48	70	90
Mos Def	Murphy Lee	Jay-Z
50	72	92
DMX	Pimp C.	M.I.A.
52	74	
Styles P	Method Man	
54	76	
Jim Jones	Ol' Dirty Bastard	

FOREWORD

There aren't many things I remember from my childhood as clearly as I remember my first encounters with hip-hop. I feel lucky to be old enough to have witnessed its beginning and old enough to understand it. I am also lucky to have been born and raised in the Bronx at the time. The term "hip-hop purist" was created for someone like me. There is no greater time in hip-hop than its beginning. I heard the underground tapes in grade school. We would gather around boomboxes like people gathered around radios listening to war reports during World War II. In 1980 we moved from Twin Parks in the South Bronx to the brand new River Park Towers high-rise apartments, over-looking the East River just north of Yankee Stadium. Across the street was Cedar Park where hip-hop, in essence, was born. That same year, at age twelve, I remember getting *Rapper's Delight* as a gift from my mother's friend. I remember sleeping with my first pair of British Walkers under my pillow. I remember going down to Canal Street looking for dyed sheepskins. Hip-hop defined me.

Mike Schreiber and I met at a time when, for me, hip-hop had become the force working against my creativity. I was a stubborn artist balking at every opportunity that came my way in the name of holding on to my artistic freedom. It had to be in the waiting room of *The Source* or *VIBE*. We hit it off immediately and became fast friends. To this day our conversations range from religion to race, politics, the disappearing traditions of media and debating about who is the top MC of the moment.

Mike's pictures evoke the same deep-rooted feelings I have for my culture of hip-hop. Not the reflection of its own glossy desire but the representation of its true grit and worth. The innocence of a Lil Wayne, the comedy of Biz Markie, the fun loving Big Pun, the brotherhood of Black Star's Mos Def and Talib Kweli, the stoicism of Eminem. Hip-hop needs a Mike Schreiber to tell its truth because when all the bling and gloss and desire fade it will still stand because of its honesty.

Craig "muMs" Grant is a New York City-based writer and actor born and raised in the Bronx. He is best known for his role as "Poet" in the HBO prison-drama OZ. *His performances have led to many roles in TV and film. As a performance poet, muMs has performed internationally at over 150 colleges and universities. As a writer, his short film* Morning Breath *won honorable mention at the Sundance Film Festival and his latest work, the play* Paradox of the Urban Cliché, *was produced by the LAByrinth Theater Company, which muMs has been a member of since 2006.*

INTRODUCTION

I worked as a photo editor at a celebrity photo agency in the mid-'90s, checking out the negatives and prints brought in by the photographers. I knew I liked concerts and I liked taking pictures. More importantly, I realized that these photographers weren't doing anything that I couldn't do. So I learned how to get photo passes to shows and, through trial (and much error), I started shooting concerts. Some of the agency photographers got nervous and complained to my boss. He told me that I had to stop shooting or I'd be fired.

I got fired.

I was shooting a lot, but wasn't making any money. So I set up some job interviews at other photo agencies. Midway through the second interview, I realized that I *really* didn't want to get the job. It was at that moment that I decided to figure out how to make a living as a photographer.

I signed on with an agency to syndicate my pictures (still don't know why they decided to sign me) and set about getting myself into shows. I gravitated to hip-hop because I dug the music, plus getting into shows was easier and backstage access was a breeze.

I shot as much as I could at places like Tramps, Wetlands and Roseland, and the day after shooting I'd get my film processed and head over to *The Source* and *VIBE* to try and get the previous night's pictures placed in their party pages. I'd call the magazines and ask to be connected to whomever handled those particular pages, like Riggs at *The Source* and Shani at *VIBE*. This was before email, so I'd call, tell them what I had and if they were interested I'd bring them the pics. *The Source* paid $85 per picture and *VIBE* paid $60, so if I placed three or four in each magazine,

I knew my rent would be paid for the month. Once I started getting pictures placed regularly, publicists took notice and would start inviting me to record release parties and such, sometimes paying me to shoot at them. This was my hustle for a few years.

Shooting shows was fun, but it was also exhausting, and when I found out how much money photographers made for album packages and advertising jobs, I realized that I had to switch up my game and figure out how to shoot more portraits.

I didn't have any real training (I studied anthropology in school) and I never assisted, so I learned as I went along. When I was a kid, cameras and picture taking were always part of everyday life. My grandpa Manny was a big picture guy, and I recently saw some really great photos that my dad took when he was younger. My dad even had a little darkroom set up in the bathroom. To this day, my mom always has a camera with her.

I always loved drawing and painting and taking candid pictures of family and friends. It wasn't until college, though, that I really started shooting (I worked for the school paper). And it wasn't until after college that I realized that it was possible to make a living as a photographer.

People always ask me about what inspires me. I always tell them that my main inspiration comes from an overwhelming desire to never have a regular job. Twelve years in, and so far so good.

This book is a culmination of my hustle and all the love I've received along the way.

Mike Schreiber is a self-taught New York City photographer with a degree in anthropology from the University of Connecticut. His work has been featured in Esquire, Rolling Stone, TRACE, New York magazine, VIBE, XXL, SLAM, SPIN and Arise. Schreiber has shot ad campaigns for Mountain Dew, AND-t, City Year and Partnership For A Drug-Free America. His other clients include Atlantic Records, Epic Records, Sony, Universal Records and Koch Records.

Schreiber's work captures varied subjects including entertainers, prisoners in Angola state prison and kids on the streets of Cuba. His humanistic approach to life is reflected in the full gallery of mostly black and white photographs. His photos capture the true essence of cultural life and perspective, resulting in an unparalleled aesthetic viewpoint that is refined yet undeniably honest in its raw and gritty tone.

Biz Markie

12

Biz Markie

Prince Paul

I was shooting Prince Paul for *Mass Appeal* magazine. We were in my East Village apartment and he was telling me stories about being a member of Stetsasonic (an early Brooklyn hip-hop crew known for inspirational lyrics and performing with live bands), getting free Knicks tickets and being treated like New York City royalty. This particular picture was one of the last I shot that day—just Paul up against my living room wall. Simple but cool. It's one of my favorites.

Slick Rick

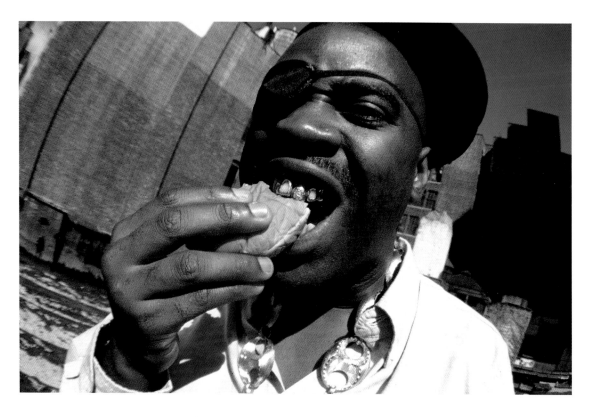

The British magazine *Hip-Hop Connection* asked me to shoot Slick Rick for a cover. I'd been sending them slides for a long time (this was way before email), trying to sell them my work.

It was my first cover shoot, so I went and rented a giant camera that I didn't know how to load and a light meter that I didn't know how to use. (I didn't study photography in school, and I never assisted, so my technical skills were extremely limited.)

We shot in my apartment on 26th Street. It was surreal having Slick Rick and his wife in my living room with my dog and roommates coming in and out. It wasn't the most professional situation, but I didn't know any better. And he was real cool. Easy breezy.

True Hip-Hop

De La Soul

True Hip-Hop

Flavor Flav (with Nigo, founder of clothing line Bape)

True Hip-Hop

True Hip-Hop

True Hip-Hop

The Source sent me out to California to shoot the Up in Smoke tour, which featured Eminem, Snoop, Dr. Dre, Ice Cube and Xzibit. I was supposed to travel with the tour from Anaheim to Sacramento with full backstage access and everything. It didn't really turn out that way though because nobody from the magazine bothered to ask for permission or to tell anyone from the tour about our plans.

The writer and I got to the venue in Anaheim without tickets or a photo pass waiting for us. Calls were made, and somehow we were able to get into the show, but I didn't have permission to shoot. All I remember from that show is that the writer somehow got himself kicked out of the arena. That was funny.

By the time we got to Sacramento, permission to take photos was secured, but only for one song during each artist's performance. I don't remember much about Sacramento other than that there was a fireman's convention at the hotel we were staying in, so there were lots of burly mustachioed men drinking beer in the hotel's hot tub all day and night. That was strange. We were in Sacramento for a few days with nothing to do (the pool was full of firemen and the women who love them). I called the photo editor to try and get an earlier ticket for my return trip. She told me it was too expensive, but that I should go to the beach or something. We were in Sacramento. There are no beaches in Sacramento. I was happy to come home.

True Hip-Hop

Eminem

The Source had a page called "Unsigned Hype" where unsigned artists would send in their demo tapes; if the editors liked them, they'd be that month's "Unsigned Hype" artist. At the time, artists were sending in their own pictures with their tapes, and most of the pictures were really, really bad. I saw an opportunity, so I called the photo editor and offered to shoot "Unsigned Hype" for free. I figured the pictures I took wouldn't be worse than the ones sent in by the artists, and it'd be a good opportunity for me to do some portraits without much pressure. The editor agreed and said I could shoot the next New York City-based artist.

The third "Unsigned Hype" portrait I did was of a white kid from Detroit named Eminem. His manager's cousin owned a studio so we shot there. He was dope. Real humble and quiet. Within a year he was on the cover of *Rolling Stone*.

True Hip-Hop

Young Buck

XXL sent me to Nashville to shoot Young Buck. The thing about southern cities is that once you get off the tourist strip, things get real serious real fast. Gangs tag all the corners and stop signs to show who controls the block. Buck was driving us around the day before the shoot, showing us the sights, scouting locations and telling us about how the day before a kid had been found with his face shot off. Good times.

After the session, Buck wanted me to get some shots of him with his crew. I agreed and we decided to use a stoop in front of the projects. To get the angle I wanted I had to get on top of a truck. It had rained the day before and it was muddy. Climbing up I lost my footing and fell in the mud. Everyone thought it was hilarious. I wasn't really in a position to argue, so I got back up on the truck and shot the picture.

Buck was playing music in his truck the entire time we were shooting, so by the end of the day his battery died and he had to get it jumped by the police.

Dwele

36

True Hip-Hop

Maino

I shot Juelz in front of Keith Haring's *Crack Is Wack* mural on 128th Street. Juelz asked me to shoot it so that the words "crack is wack" wouldn't be seen.

43

Mos Def and Talib Kweli bought a bookstore in Brooklyn called Nkiru Books and *The Source* assigned me to shoot them in front of the store. I knew both of them from Lyricist Lounge, so I was excited to do it.

I showed up on time but they weren't there yet, so I took some pictures of the store and waited. Then I waited some more. I seem to remember Kweli showing up, waiting for a bit and then leaving.

After waiting for a long time, I knew that I could either leave or wait some more... so I waited some more.

Mos finally showed up (and Kweli returned) and I took a few pictures of them in front of the store. Then I asked to do some individual portraits. This wasn't part of the assignment, but after waiting so long I wanted to make sure it was worth my time. Nobody was really giving me assignments to shoot portraits at the time so I really needed to take what was in front of me and get the most out of every opportunity.

The funny thing about this picture is that the assignment wasn't really to shoot Mos Def. I'm sure the editors would have been okay with just pictures of the bookstore. I literally waited hours for him to show up. I'm glad my ego didn't take over that day, because if it had, I would have left and never would have taken this picture (next spread).

Mos Def

True Hip-Hop

Jim Jones

C. Murder

XXL flew me down to Mississippi to shoot David Banner. This was before his first album came out, so I didn't know what he looked like. After my plane landed, I got my rental car and called him to find out where to meet. He sounded incredulous, and asked me where I was. I told him I was in the rental car at the airport. He told me he was at the airport, too. Said he'd come to pick me up! This was a first.

We drove around town, shot in front of a broken down building and an abandoned mental hospital. Then we went to his mom's house. He decided he wanted neighborhood kids in the shots, so he started going around, knocking on neighbors' doors and asking if the kids could come out to be in a photo. So we had all the neighborhood kids out for a photo.

Then I took some pictures of him on the back of a pickup truck and we decided it'd be great if he threw a brick at me (for the photo, not out of malice).

I flew out that night and was back in New York around 8:00 p.m. A couple hours later I got a call from a number I didn't recognize. It was Mr. Banner, sounding worried and a little annoyed. He was calling to make sure I got home safely and he was kind of upset that I hadn't called to let him know that I'd made it home.

One of the best people I've met in hip-hop.

Lil Wayne

Young Jeezy

Murphy Lee

True Hip-Hop

Pimp C.

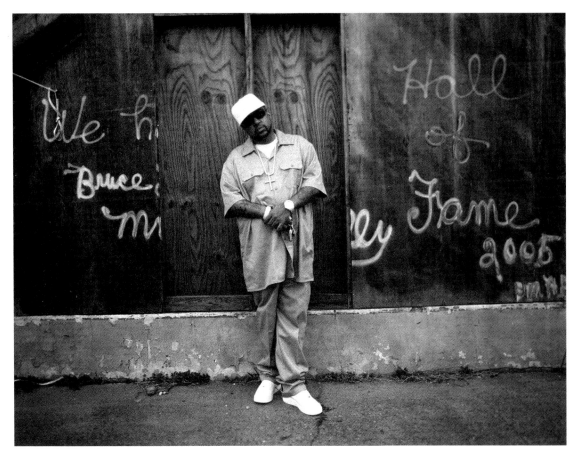

While shooting Pimp C. in front of his home in Port Arthur, Texas, his dad came home from work, wearing jeans and a baseball cap. When we asked him if he wanted to be in the magazine, he went in the house and came out with his cowboy hat. I like this picture because even with the obvious generational gap in the way they dress and carry themselves, there's clearly love between them.

When I found out that Pimp C. had died, the first thing I thought of was his dad and how sad he must have been.

73

I was in Harlem, shooting Method Man and Bobbito for *VIBE*. When Meth arrived he looked around at all of the new buildings and their occupants and shouted: "This ain't Harlem! This ain't Harlem!" Like in a movie, a random crackhead rolled up and, even more loudly than Meth, declared: "YOOOOOO... METHOD MAN!!! I used to smoke with you in Staten Island in '93!" Meth gave him a pound and turned to everyone and said, "This is Harlem... this still Harlem."

The crackhead ended up working "security," maintaining a tight perimeter around us throughout the shoot so nobody bothered Meth or interfered with any of the shots. When I was done shooting for the magazine I told the crackhead that it was cool to let the people mingle freely. Meth signed these kids' hands, which made for a dope shot. As we were wrapping up the crackhead offered to walk Meth across the street to his car, and I overheard him asking for some money. Dude told him he was collecting for his church.

Ol' Dirty Bastard

True Hip-Hop

I shot the Jungle Brothers for Gee Street Records at the Great Day in Hip-Hop event in Harlem. I spent the day running around taking pictures of everyone there and as I was walking back to the train I noticed this guy sitting on a stoop. He looked a lot like Redman. I stopped and asked if I could take his picture. Then I asked him why he wasn't at the event. He told me that nobody told him about it. I thought it was kind of strange that he just happened to be sitting on a stoop half a block away from the event, claiming to not know that it was happening. Some questions are better left not asked. I took a few photographs of him and went home.

True Hip-Hop

Diddy

True Hip-Hop

For *XXL*, I shot Ms. Wallace at her house in the Poconos. She is incredibly warm and genuine. I really liked her, and it made me sad that the only reason I was taking her picture was because her son had been murdered.

She had B.I.G.'s "money green leather sofa" in her living room and pictures of her son and grandkids all over the house.

She told us about how she'd throw rocks at the deer when they'd try to eat her flowers.

This is one of my favorite portraits.

True Hip-Hop

I shot State Property for *XXL* in DUMBO, Brooklyn, in an area popular for photo shoots. My brother was helping me out that day. He and I were in the location van waiting for the group to show up when none other than Nas climbs into the van and asks where he can change clothes.

This was at the height of the Jay-Z/Nas beef, so I was shitting myself and hoping that he'd be gone before Beanie Sigel and his crew rolled up. It turned out that Nas was doing a shoot for another magazine a few blocks from where we were, and he saw the location van and assumed it was for him. He left a few minutes before State Property showed up, thankfully.

Jay-Z

This is back from when I was mostly shooting live stuff. I've shot Jay in concert a few times, and this image is from a show he did at the Apollo Theatre. The show was amazing. The Apollo is fairly small and every single person knew every single word to every single song. The atmosphere was electric! At the end of the show Jay had a little ceremony for the newest member of the Roc-A-Fella family: Kanye West.

I was taking pictures of my friend in her loft in Williamsburg, Brooklyn, when I got a phone call from the photo editor at *URB* magazine. She asked me if I'd like to shoot an artist named M.I.A. for the cover of their up-and-coming artists issue. The only catch was that it had to be shot the next day, and I needed to come up with a location. This was 2005, and I'd never heard of M.I.A., but it was for the cover so I told the editor that I'd be happy to do the shoot. I asked my friend if I could shoot M.I.A. in her apartment the next day. She said okay.

M.I.A. was real cool. No stylist, just her and her clothing. We shot a bunch of portraits for the cover. I noticed this giant boombox sitting in my friend's living room and we went up to the roof with it.

The funny thing about this picture is that it almost didn't happen. I remember M.I.A.'s publicist kept telling me that we had to wrap it up because they had to get to another photo shoot. Both women were real cool though, and they let me keep shooting until I thought I was done.

I've shot her twice since then, but that day was particularly special. M.I.A. is definitely at the top of my list of favorite subjects. I'd love to shoot her every day!

ACKNOWLEDGMENTS

To both my parents. To Dad for showing me how to treat people, both in professional and personal life; the best advice he ever gave me was to start every conversation with a smile. I think that's been my greatest tool as a photographer. And thanks to Mom for nurturing my creativity and allowing me to explore and for never trying to change me.

And thanks to everyone who gave me opportunities and chances to shoot when I didn't even have a portfolio.

Peace to Blue in Heaven.